P9-ARB-583

Isaac Cruikshank's DRAWINGS FOR DROLLS

Isaac Cruikshank's
DRAWINGS FOR DROLLS

with an Introduction and Notes by ROBERT R. WARK

THE HUNTINGTON LIBRARY · SAN MARINO, CALIFORNIA

1968

Acknowledgment

I am indebted to Mary Dorothy George, Wilmarth Lewis, Eleanor Nicholes of The Widener Collection, and Reginald Williams of The British Museum for assistance in connection with this study. I also wish to thank Ann Ely and Nancy Moll of the Huntington Library for their help in preparing the material for the printer. The publication was made possible through the generosity of C F Braun & Co and the Trustees of the Huntington Library.

R.R.W.

Library of Congress Catalog Card Number 68-31202
Printed and designed by C F Braun & Co

Cover: 48. CHARMS OF PRECEDENCE

Introduction

It is a happy occasion when a major cache of the works of even a minor artist reappears after a long period in hiding, especially when this material serves to establish the artist's reputation on a higher plane than it has previously enjoyed. The group of drawings discussed in this little book form quantitatively the largest and qualitatively the best collection of the sketches by Isaac Cruikshank now recorded. They stretch chronologically over a major portion of his career, and they considerably enlarge our knowledge of his work as a comic draftsman. Although they have never been literally lost, and their history can be traced back to the early nineteenth century, their whereabouts seems to have been unknown and even their existence generally forgotten during the past fifty years.

Isaac Cruikshank is an artist whose name appears in virtually every book concerned with English comic art. He merits this position in his own right, but the attention is also to a considerable extent a reflection of the luster that surrounds his son George, probably the most famous English illustrator of the nineteenth century. Isaac himself is a shadowy figure, and even the recent appearance of a monograph, the first ever to be written on the artist, has not really dispelled much of the mist. We know next to nothing about his life. He apparently was not considered important enough to warrant an obituary biographical notice in contemporary periodicals such as the *Gentleman's Magazine*. It was not until over half a century after his death that Samuel Redgrave gave the first connected account of his life, and this (in the *Dictionary of Artists of the English School*) consists of only one hundred and fifty words.

A little more biographical information has come to light as a result of research promoted by the late Dr. E. B. Krumbhaar and embodied in his monograph on Isaac. It now seems reasonably certain that the artist was born at Edinburgh on October 5, 1764, rather than in 1756 or 1757 as was previously thought. But we still have no definite information about his family background and upbringing. His father, Andrew, is said to have been a customhouse officer and a Jacobite who turned to art after losing his position following the uprising of 1745; he also is supposed to have died when Isaac, the youngest of his five offspring, was still a child. Isaac appears in London by 1784 as an engraver and printseller, but his output during the eighties seems to have been small and his personality as an artist not as yet clearly formed.

Probably shortly after his arrival in London he married a Scottish girl, Mary McNaughton, a sensible and businesslike woman who helped her husband in his trade and bore him two sons, Robert and George, as well as a daughter who died young. The whole family was interested in art and seems to have cooperated in the preparation of the engraved plates for which Isaac provided the designs. The Cruikshanks enjoyed moderate prosperity. Isaac was socially inclined and (like many of his fellow artists) is supposed to have been prone to drinking bouts with his friends. But, as his wife boasted in later life that she had been able to put aside the then considerable sum of one thousand pounds, she must have kept her husband's convivial tendencies under control.

The peak of Isaac's artistic career seems to have been the mid-1790's, judging from the number of prints by him (mostly political caricatures) assigned to those years in the British Museum *Catalogue of Political and Personal Satires*. He continued moderately active through the first decade of the nineteenth century but ceased to produce about 1810. In spite of thorough researches initiated by Dr. Krumbhaar, no information concerning the date of Isaac's death has been found. Redgrave (who was in a position to check such information with the family) states he died about 1810 as the result of a severe cold. Some prints bearing his name appeared in 1811, but these may easily have been executed several months before they were published.

Isaac's active career was thus about twenty-five years, from 1784 to 1810, with most of his work coming after 1790. For practical purposes his total known output lies within the general area of comic draftsmanship. He did exhibit at the Royal Academy on three occasions (1789, 1790, 1792). The pictures are not known to have survived, but the titles suggest that Isaac may in these instances have aspired to the status of a narrative genre painter. These items aside, everything else we know of him indicates that his interests remained with caricature and comic art.

With two exceptions all of the Huntington drawings by Isaac are contained in a single large folio volume. A fair amount of information concerning this book is at hand. The drawings, all carefully inset into larger pages, were bound together by John Hering, who is known to have been active during the 1830's and 1840's; one of the endpapers carries a Whatman

GEORGE CRUIKSHANK'S FRONTISPIECE FOR THE HUNTINGTON VOLUME OF ISAAC'S DROLLS

watermark for 1839. The drawings were apparently bound for a certain William Knight of Canonbury, and the volume was included in his sale at Sotheby's in August of 1847 (lot 1365). During the late nineteenth century the drawings belonged to Sir William Augustus Fraser of Ledeclune and appeared again at Sotheby's in his sale during April of 1901 (lot 473). At that time they were purchased by the dealer Sabin, from whom they apparently passed to the collection of F. R. Halsey. Mr. Huntington purchased this last library en bloc in 1915.

Bound in with the volume is a frontispiece especially provided by George Cruikshank. It is a sketch of his father at work at his drawing table with young George standing beside him. The drawing is attractive and has added interest as a rare representation of Isaac (although the view shows more of the back of his head than the front). If, as seems probable, the portrait on the wall in the background of the sketch is also meant to be Isaac, then he and his son George must have resembled each other closely. More important than the drawing itself is an inscription below it by George reading as follows: "The Drawings in this Book are all by my deceased Father Isaac Cruikshank, with the exception of the few marked as not being by him—The greater part of these drawings were made when I was a boy, and whilst standing by his side. I can thus speak to their authenticity, and have great pleasure in certifying it, to my friend William Knight Esq. of Canonbury. George Cruikshank."

There is a total of one hundred and sixteen drawings in the volume, in addition to the frontispiece. Four of these George has designated as not by his father, and it is quite clear even on casual examination that they are indeed the work of other hands. The remaining drawings, although they exhibit considerable variety, are sufficiently consistent that one has no difficulty in accepting them as all by the same artist. It is true that in later life George is known to have given somewhat conflicting statements concerning his own early work and his father's. But the inscription in the Huntington volume must date at the latest from the mid-1840's when George was still in full control of his faculties, and there seems no reason to doubt the information he gives us concerning the drawings.

A few of the sketches are signed, and a few are dated. Nearly all have inscriptions on the backs giving a title and Isaac Cruikshank's name, but this information appears not to be in Isaac's handwriting. The internal evidence offered by the drawings themselves is insufficient to cope with the numerous problems they present. But fortunately investigation has estab-

2. TIGHT BOOTS

lished that the majority (and probably in fact all) are preparatory to engravings. Prints based on ninety-eight of the drawings have now been located. Very few of them bear Isaac's name, although Mrs. George, in her *Catalogue of Political and Personal Satires . . . in the British Museum*, was astute enough to suspect that several were his work. Most of the prints, however, have been treated as anonymous. Nearly all the prints are dated and bear explanatory titles and inscriptions. It is logical to assume that the drawings are close in date to the prints based on them. The prints thus provide both a chronological framework and information concerning subject matter when dealing with the drawings.

All of the engraved drawings in the volume (including those designated by George Cruikshank as not by his father) were issued by the printseller Robert Sayer and (after mid-1794) by his successors in trade, Laurie and Whittle, who purchased his stock. The prints all appeared in a series known as "Drolls," a word apparently used at the time for humorous, non-political sketches. A catalog issued by Laurie and Whittle in 1795 contains a list of many of these prints and describes them as follows: "Quarto Drolls, eight inches high, by ten wide, consisting of the greatest variety of whimsical, satirical and burlesque subjects, (but not political,) They are well calculated for the shop windows of country booksellers and stationers, etc. One shilling each coloured, six-pence plain."

The general idea behind the prints is very close to our single-picture cartoon, a normal feature of most modern daily newspapers and weekly magazines. There is always at least a title, and frequently several lines of explanation. The humor is often carried by the caption, but in the more successful examples the picture and the explanation supplement each other for the comic effect. One would, of course, like very much to know whether the captions were supplied by Isaac himself or suggested to him; but there is no answer to this question at present. The humor is not subtle or sophisticated, and is often on the vulgar side.

There is a considerable range for the topics touched on in the drawings, although the themes generally are all frequent in the comic art of the period. Sex and marriage, perennial favorites, occur probably more often than any other subjects. Various professional, social, and national types are also recurring butts for humor, as are any extremes of fashion, particularly in dress. The comic mishap or situation, which is so popular a theme with Thomas Rowlandson, occurs less frequently in the works of Isaac but is certainly there on occasion. One must admit, however, there is

21. A FRENCH EMIGRANT COOK BEGGING FOR A SLICE OF ENGLISH BEEF

often nothing inherently funny about the drawing at all, and the humor is carried entirely by the text. There are several instances of verbal puns; and one suspects these may be more frequent than is now apparent, especially in the play between a proper and a vulgar or slang use of a word. In other instances the text relates a joke or humorous tale for which the design is simply an illustration.

The type of comic art to which Cruikshank's Drolls belong has a history in England going back at least half a century before Isaac's involvement with it. As an art form it often goes hand in hand with political caricature, and most of the artists active in one also practiced in the other. But the artists themselves seem to have made a distinction between these two forms of comic draftsmanship. The political caricatures were apparently regarded as more ephemeral. The preliminary drawings for them are often no more than hasty pencil notations worked up quickly (one suspects) to take advantage of a particular political situation and produced as prints while this situation was still news. Such sketches by Isaac for political caricatures as are now known tend to be of this type. On the other hand, comic drawings of a more general nature were frequently developed with much greater care and deliberation. They were normally executed in pen and enriched with watercolors, and they were clearly intended to have value and existence as independent works of art apart from the prints that were based on them. All of the drawings by Isaac in the Huntington collection are of this more elaborate type.

By the end of the eighteenth century, comic art comparable to the Cruikshank Drolls enjoyed wide popularity in England. Rowlandson comes first to mind as the greatest and most prolific practitioner in this genre. Gillray, so outstanding in political caricature, was less concerned with this more general area of comic art. But other men like Bunbury, Dighton, Nixon, Boyne, Woodward, and Newton produced quantities of lively pen and watercolor drawings of humorous subjects with no specific political implications.

This rather elegant and decorative comic drawing seems to be French in origin and was probably brought to England by a number of artists of French training or extraction. But the idea fell on particularly fertile ground in England and was developed as an art form far beyond anything one finds on the other side of the Channel. Hogarth, generally regarded as the fountainhead of English comic art, never produced this type of elegant exhibition drawing. His sketches,

22. THE OLD BATCHELOR ALARMED BY AN UNEXPECTED PRESENT

powerful as they frequently are, normally are in pencil or pen and are intended either as notations for his own reference or as working drawings for the engraver, rather than as self-contained works of art. Nevertheless, Hogarth clearly anticipates virtually the whole range of humor that subsequently appears in English comic art, and plumbs the national inclination in this direction.

Drawings that anticipate more closely the visual effect of the comic pen and watercolor sketch begin to appear in England about the middle of the eighteenth century. Louis Philippe Boitard (son of the better-known François Boitard) was producing drawings of London street characters about 1740-50 that are at least technically close to the work of Rowlandson and Cruikshank forty years later. We know very little about Boitard's training, but he presumably learned this technique in France. His drawings, however, are not always aiming for a specifically comic effect. Closer to the mark are a few sketches by Charles Brandoin (apparently identical with Michel Vincent Brandoin), who spent some time in England during the 1760's and 70's. There is in particular a drawing by him in the Huntington collection representing the Royal Academy Exhibition of 1771 which anticipates exactly the type of comic drawing that became so popular in England in the two following decades. Probably more important, because he remained in England for most of his career, was the French-trained Philip de Loutherbourg, who likewise was producing drawings during the 1770's that are of much the same type as Rowlandson's sketches of the 1780's. Of course, Rowlandson himself spent some time in France during the 1770's, and his contact with this form of art might equally well have been at its source. But whatever the channels by which it reached England, the immediate origins of the comic pen and watercolor drawing would appear to be French.

Isaac Cruikshank can hardly be regarded as in the van of those concerned with this developing interest in humorous art. We hear nothing of him as a designer until the mid-1780's, by which time Rowlandson, although still in his twenties, had already produced some of his most brilliant and popular designs. It is not until about 1790 that Isaac emerges clearly as an artist in his own right, and by then nearly all the principal practitioners of comic draftsmanship in England are in full flower.

Judging by the prints based on them, the drawings by Isaac in the Huntington collection date between 1790 and 1804. There are drawings which may be assigned to each year except 1802 and 1803, with the ma-

27. JUSTICE MITTIMUS AT A LOSS HOW TO ACT IN THIS AFFAIR

jor concentrations coming in 1794 and 1798. The last half-dozen years of Isaac's career are not represented, but the period that is covered amounts to nearly three quarters of his active life. The drawings thus provide a particularly interesting opportunity to study the evolution of his style and artistic personality. To be sure, there are no very startling developments. But his manner of drawing does change perceptibly, and it is possible to distinguish at least three style phases in the works here included.

The earliest of the drawings, from 1790, 1791, and 1792, are frequently in monochrome wash. Color, when it does appear, is subdued in effect and may be limited to a few areas, such as the faces and hands. The contours are often sketchy in treatment and are not accentuated. Generally the drawings have a loose, sometimes rather woolly appearance.

In the mid-1790's the contour lines begin to take on a more positive character; the colors become brighter and are used with stronger decorative effect. In 1794, which seems to have been Isaac's true vintage year as far as these drawings are concerned, the contours become comparatively broad and flexible. They appear to be drawn with a much coarser reed pen than heretofore, or possibly even with a brush. They are strong and black, outlining the figures and color areas clearly, creating a visual effect very much more lively and vigorous than in the earlier drawings. The colors make an important contribution to this effect and are frequently applied in rather large areas, distributed with some care over the surface of the picture.

As the decade progresses, Isaac's drawing appears to become tighter and more wiry. He models more with color. The figures themselves become more doll-like and are frequently smaller in scale relative to the rest of the picture than they were earlier. These tendencies crystallize in a large group of drawings belonging to 1798, sketches that are thoroughly competent but more dry and mechanical in general effect than those of 1794.

The impression created by the drawings after 1798 is that Isaac was becoming careless and slipshod. There are accomplished sketches with the rather tight competence of those of 1798, but there are also others where the drawing is sloppy, the color crude, and the general effect garish.

The artistic personality that emerges from the group as a whole is reasonably consistent but not highly individual. One suspects that Cruikshank had an eye on what his competitors were doing and was likely influenced by them. And yet in fairness to Isaac it should be said that there is sometimes uncertainty about

29. A SPOUTING CLUB

which way the influence worked. The rather coarse, flexible, reed-pen outline that is noticeable in the drawings of 1794 is often associated with the amateurs Woodward and Bunbury. Isaac had close connections with Woodward and engraved many plates based on his drawings. But the peak of this collaboration was in 1795, well after Isaac had developed a style that resembles Woodward's. Rowlandson used a similarly vigorous and flexible pen line during the 1780's and early 1790's but was already modifying this technique before Isaac adopted it. Rowlandson and Isaac both tend to develop a tighter, more wiry line in their work after the mid-1790's, and indeed both tend to become much more uneven and careless artists in their later years. But it seems likely that these parallel developments are the result of parallel circumstances (pressures of printmaking, tendencies to produce potboilers, all aggravated by convivial habits) rather than of any interinfluence.

Isaac cannot, of course, withstand direct comparison with Rowlandson. He lacks the older man's astonishing virtuosity as a draftsman and especially the highly personal bouncy calligraphy which is the vehicle for "Rowly's" infectious good humor. Nor does he have Rowlandson's keen eye for the genuinely comic in the purely visual sense. Isaac's visual imagination and invention in pictorial organization are far outdistanced by Gillray, although the latter preferred to direct his savage humor against political topics rather than the type of subject Isaac treated in his Drolls. But these two giants aside, Cruikshank (as revealed through the Huntington drawings) appears to hold his own with any of his numerous contemporaries in the field of comic art. His sketches at their best are amusing, vigorous, and decorative and much more lively simply as drawings than the rather mechanical prints based on them would suggest. It should be admitted, however, that the drawings of many of the other comic draftsmen (as distinct from their prints) are rare, and their personalities no better known than that of Isaac before the reemergence of the drawings for Drolls. One hopes there may be many other such caches awaiting rediscovery, to provide for our enjoyment and increase our understanding of this highly entertaining and ingratiating phase of British art.

52. MONSIEUR TONSON

Catalog

All the drawings listed in this catalog except numbers 113 and 114 were acquired in 1915 in the single volume described in the Introduction. While these sketches form much the largest group now known of Isaac's drawings for Drolls, it is clear that the series is not complete. The problem of identifying other sketches for the series is complicated by the fact that no complete file of the engravings or even any full list of the titles is recorded. Among the small number of drawings by Isaac in public collections other than the Huntington, there is one in the Victoria and Albert Museum that can be identified as for the Drolls (George 10350). Another drawing for the series was with J. S. Maas in 1968 (George 8923). There was a substantial group of Isaac's drawings (mostly political caricatures) in the William H. Woodin collection (sold at Parke-Bernet, December 1941 and January and February 1942). Many of these entered the collection of the late Dr. E. B. Krumbhaar and are listed in his monograph on Isaac; a few of these may be for the Drolls.

The three principal collections of engravings of the Drolls used in connection with this study are referred to by the following abbreviations:

George: Mary Dorothy George, *Catalogue of Political and Personal Satires Preserved in the Department of Prints and Drawings in the British Museum*, Vol. VI (1938), Vol. VII (1942), Vol. VIII (1947).

LWL: The Lewis Walpole Library, Farmington, Connecticut.

WMC: The Widener Collection in the Harvard College Library.

The titles given to the drawings in this catalog follow those on the prints when these are known.

The arrangement is as far as possible chronological, following the dates of publication where these are known.

78. CAPTAIN WATTLE AND MISS ROE

1. TAKING WATER FOR VAUXHALL

Pen and watercolor; 7″ x 8⅝″
Inscribed verso: Taking water for Vauxhall / I. Cruikshanks
Published: 1790 by Robert Sayer
George 7801

A young man helps a young woman into a boat held by a young waterman. The lady lifts her skirt, exposing her ankle.

On the print beneath the title is engraved:
Be cautious my Love—don't expose your leg.

2. TIGHT BOOTS

Pen and monochrome gray wash, with touches of color in the faces and hands; 7″ x 8⅞″
Signed: Cruikshanks 1790
Inscribed verso: Tight boots / I. Cruikshanks
No print after this drawing has been located.

A rather disheveled man sits on a chair while two women try to take off his boots. The older woman, straddling his left leg, pulls at the left boot from the ankle. The young woman, wearing a hat, stands behind the chair holding the man's shoulders.

A print entitled "New Boots, or the Old Buck in Distress" is listed in *Laurie & Whittle's Catalogue of New and Interesting Prints* (1795), p. 97, no. 62.

3. A FOOL AND HIS MONEY'S SOON PARTED

Pen and monochrome gray wash; 6¾″ x 8¾″
Signed: Cruikshanks [partially trimmed off]
Inscribed verso: Love and Wine / I. Cruikshanks
Published: May 1, 1790, by Robert Sayer
George 7802 (Mrs. George lists this print a second time under 8406, an impression with the imprint cut off)

A middle-aged man sits on a couch fondling a young woman while a second woman picks his pocket.

There are four lines of verse on the print beginning:
The Old Booby half Muzzy, to a Bagnio Reel'd

4. NONE BUT THE BRAVE DESERVE THE FAIR

Pen and watercolor; 7″ x 8⅜″
Inscribed verso: None but the Brave / deserves the Fair / I. Cruikshanks
Published: May 1, 1790, by Robert Sayer
George 7803

A young woman, fashionably dressed in a high-crowned hat, steps between two elderly men who have their fists clenched and appear ready to fight. The man to the left is very spindly; the man to the right is on crutches. Mrs. George, in her comment on the print, assumes that the young woman is a courtesan, and this interpretation seems probably correct.

3. A FOOL AND HIS MONEY'S SOON PARTED

5. THE HUSBAND HIGHLY DELIGHTED WITH HIS SUPPOSED FRUITS

Pen and monochrome gray wash; 7″ x 8½″
Inscribed verso: The Husband delighted with his supposed Fruits / I. Cruikshanks
Published: May 1, 1790, by Robert Sayer
George 7804

An elderly man smiles at a baby he holds on his lap. A young man watches, seated at a table to the left. A young woman stands to the right holding a roast bird in a dish with her left hand, pointing with her right at a stag's head with antlers directly above the old man.

6. THE RUSTICS ALARM'D AT THE APPEARANCE OF A LONDON BUCK

Pen and watercolor; 6⅞ x 8¾″
Inscribed verso: The London Buck / I. Cruikshanks
Published: July 27, 1790, by Robert Sayer
George 7805

A tall man dressed as a "buck" of the period stands surrounded by startled yokels; to the right two men are seated beside a cottage; a boy kneels in the doorway; to the left are a woman and child; in the background are two running figures.

This curious fashion in male dress is satirized by Cruikshank in several of the drawings for Drolls.

7. STUDYING POLITICS, OR THE BON COMPANIONS

Pen and monochrome gray wash; 6⅝″ x 8¾″
Inscribed verso: Flaming Politicians / I. Cruikshanks
Published: September 15, 1790, by Robert Sayer
George 7806

Two elderly men are dozing on either side of a fireplace with a blazing fire. The man to the right, in military uniform wearing a cocked hat, has put his peg leg on the grate and the wood has caught fire. The man to the left has his elbow on a tripod table supporting a punch bowl and a lighted candle. His wig is on fire from the candle. On the wall behind is a picture inscribed "Plan of London before the Fire of 1666."

8. A SPARRING MATCH

Pen and monochrome gray wash; 7″ x 8¾″
Inscribed verso: A Sparring Match / I. Cruikshanks
Published: September 15, 1790, by Robert Sayer
George 7807

Two men in the foreground are boxing; they wear boxing gloves, short jackets, and high collars. Several men watch from the background, including one on the extreme left with a peg leg and one to the right dressed in the costume of a "buck" of the period.

The print gives no further explanation or details concerning the scene.

5. THE HUSBAND HIGHLY DELIGHTED WITH HIS SUPPOSED FRUITS

9. FOLLY OF AN OLD MAN MARRYING A YOUNG WIFE

Pen and monochrome gray wash; 7″ x 8⅝″
Signed: I. Cruikshanks
Inscribed verso: A Curtain Lecture
Published: probably 1790
George 8407. The impression cataloged by Mrs. George has the imprint cut off. She assigns it to 1793 but says "perhaps earlier." The drawing is in the style used by Isaac in 1790 and is particularly close to "A Fool and His Money's Soon Parted."

A fat man sits on the corner of a bed. A young woman in cap with breast exposed and left arm around his neck pinches his nose, while a young man (carrying his trousers and shoes) leaves by the door to the right.

A print of this subject is listed in *Laurie & Whittle's Catalogue of New and Interesting Prints* (1795), p. 97, no. 59, and is there grouped with other prints issued in 1790.

10. TELLING FORTUNES IN COFFEE GROUNDS

Pen and monochrome gray wash; 7″ x 8¾″
Inscribed verso: Telling Fortunes / I. Cruikshanks
No print after the drawing has been located; probably 1790

Two young women in mob caps are seated around a small circular tripod table on which are a tray and coffee pot. Each holds a cup, and the lady to the left is examining the grounds in hers. A young man enters by a door in the left background.

The penwork, color, and costumes in this drawing are all closely related to others of 1790 (see nos. 3, 5, 7, and 8).

A print of this subject is in the list of Quarto Drolls contained in *Laurie & Whittle's Catalogue of New and Interesting Prints* (1795), p. 97, no. 57. Its position in the list is along with other prints of 1790.

11. THE RECRUITING SERJEANT TAKEN IN, OR ALL FAIR ABOVE BOARD

Pen and monochrome gray wash; 6⅝″ x 8⅝″
Inscribed verso: The Recruiting Serjeant / I. Cruikshanks
[also on verso a slight pencil sketch of the same subject]
Published: March 10, 1791, by Robert Sayer
George 8034

The recruiting sergeant hands money to a countryman seated at a table, to whom he has also given his hat. The table conceals the fact that the countryman has a wooden leg. To the left stands a drummer and a stout man in a doorway. To the right, seated at a table, is a young man who turns, smiling, and points at the wooden leg.

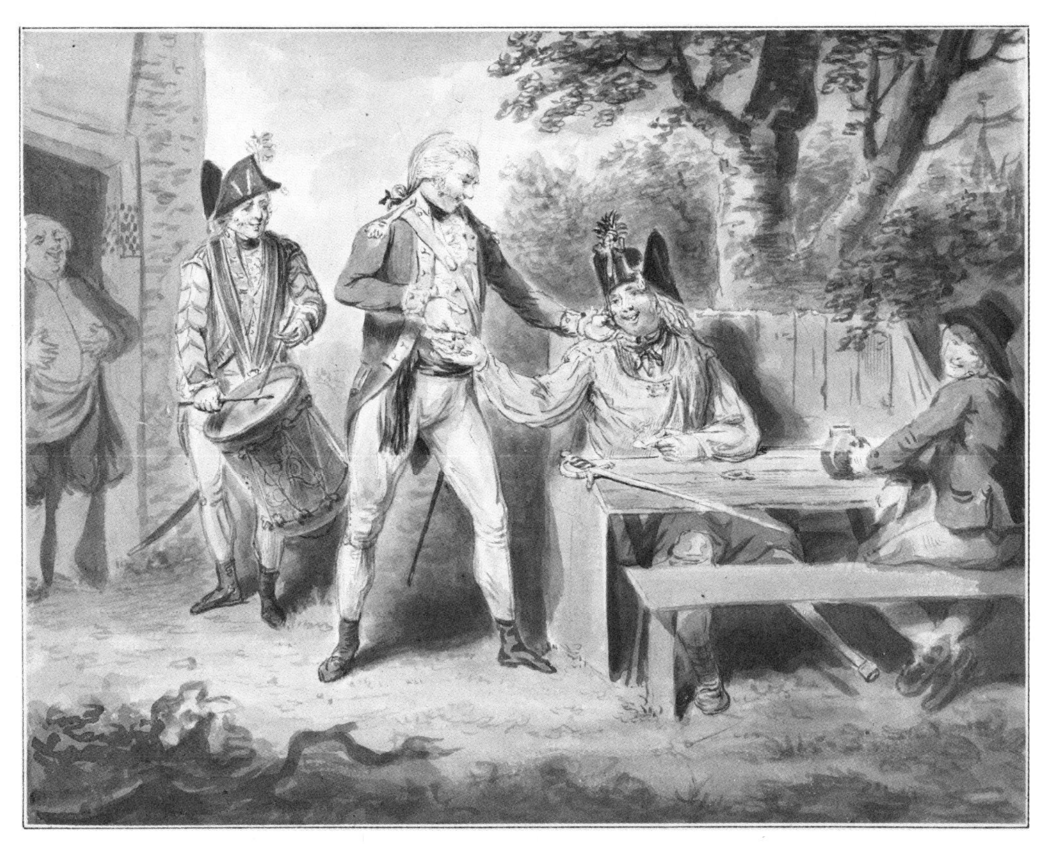

11. THE RECRUITING SERJEANT TAKEN IN, OR ALL FAIR ABOVE BOARD

12. THE ABSENT MAN

Pen and monochrome gray wash; 6⅞″ x 9¼″
Inscribed verso: The Misanthrope / I. Cruikshanks 1791
Published: January 10, 1792, by Robert Sayer
George 8212

A man walking absentmindedly in the rain steps into a pond. He has a folded umbrella under his arm, and a paper entitled "The Rights of Man" projects from his pocket. A young couple standing under a tree to the left watch and point with amusement.

13. A POINT OF HONOUR

Pen and monochrome gray wash; 6½″ x 9⅛″
Inscribed verso: A Point of Honour / I. Cruikshanks
Published: July 10, 1792, by Robert Sayer
George 8214

Two duelists stand facing each other in the middle ground. The one to the left takes aim, looking through his eyeglass. His opponent, an older man wearing spectacles and dressed in uniform, holds his pistol down. In the left foreground behind a tree trunk are two men. One, apparently a surgeon, has instruments under his arm; the other watches the duelers. In the background two heads are visible over the crest of a hill.

14. THE POLITE ALDERMAN, ADVANCING TO FUTURE HAPPINESS

Pen and monochrome gray wash; 6¾″ x 8⅝″
Inscribed verso: The polite Alderman / I. Cruikshanks
Published: August 1, 1792, by Robert Sayer
George 8215

A very stout lady and gentleman bow to one another. The lady carries a large muff from which peeks a small dog. The man, carrying a cane, has doffed his hat. A dog follows him.

Beneath the title on the print is engraved:
Madam will you honor me with your hand at the Lord Mayors Ball – With a great Deal of pleasure Mr. Alderman.

15. THE RABBITS

Pen and watercolor; 8⅞″ x 6½″
Inscribed verso: Buying Rabbits / I. Cruikshanks [also] Buckra
Published: October 8, 1792, by Robert Sayer
George 8217

A Negro selling rabbits kneels with a basket before the door of a house. A young woman standing in the door holds a rabbit by a hind foot; a man stands behind her with a finger to his nose.

14. THE POLITE ALDERMAN, ADVANCING TO FUTURE HAPPINESS

On the print the following is engraved:
Miss—O la how it smells—sure its not fresh.
Mungo—Be gar Misse dat no fair—If Blacke Man take you by Leg so—you smell too.

Mrs. George points out, in her comment on the print, that Mungo (from Bickerstaffe's *Padlock*, 1768) was a generic name for Negro.

16. LADIES EARS BORED, GRATIS

Pen and watercolor; 6¾″ x 9″
Inscribed verso: Ladies Ears Bored—gratis / I. Cruikshanks
Published: October 24, 1793, by Robert Sayer
George 8408

A woman sits in the center, her face and hands expressing dismay. A man on the right prepares to bore her ear lobe; the man on the left points to a box of ear-rings he is holding. In the right background a woman birches a weeping boy. To the left through a door can be seen a bagpipe player and a woman shouting.

17. VIEWING THE TRANSIT OF VENUS

Pen and watercolor; 6⅞″ x 8¾″
Inscribed verso: Viewing the Planet Venus / I. Cruikshanks
Published: December 16, 1793, by Robert Sayer
George 8410

A young lady sits on a bench out-of-doors looking through a telescope placed on a square table. A young man standing behind her views her appraisingly through his eyeglass. In the foliage to the right is a statue of a satyr.

18. THE MAN MILLINER

Pen and watercolor; 6¾″ x 9″
Inscribed verso: The Man Milliner / I. Cruikshanks
Published: December 16, 1793, by Robert Sayer
George 8413

The milliner stands to the left behind a counter, holding a yardstick. A woman stands facing him on the other side of the counter, holding the end of a ribbon in one hand and pointing with the other. Another woman seated in the right background watches with amusement from behind a fan.

Below the title on the print is engraved:
Indeed Mr. Fribble I am not to be done in this manner, your Yard is to short by an Inch.

19. A WATER PARTY

Pen and watercolor; 6⅜″ x 9″
Inscribed verso: A Water Party / I. Cruikshanks
No print after the drawing has been located; probably 1793

Three women and three men have capsized in a river. One lady (on the right) scrambles up the capsized

16. LADIES EARS BORED, GRATIS

boat to which one of the men also holds. Two men swim toward another woman submerged except for her legs and buttocks. The third woman, to the right, is supported by her outspread skirt but gestures with her hands. There are a bridge and buildings and other boats in the background.

A print entitled "A Serious Affair, which happened on the River Thames near Vauxhall" is included in *Laurie & Whittle's Catalogue of New and Interesting Prints* (1795), p. 98, no. 98. It is grouped with other prints of 1793.

20. SMART SHOES MADE TO FIT—WITHOUT A LAST

Pen and watercolor; 6½" x 8¾"
Inscribed verso: Shoes made to fit without a Last / I. Cruikshanks
Published: January 15, 1794, by Robert Sayer
George 8572

A lady wearing a cloak and carrying a muff is fitted with a shoe by a man kneeling before her. In the right background there is another group including a woman being fitted with a shoe.

On the print beneath the title is engraved:
Yes my lady They sit neat about the Quarters, they only want a little Bobbing.

21. A FRENCH EMIGRANT COOK BEGGING FOR A SLICE OF ENGLISH BEEF

Pen and watercolor; 7⅛" x 8⅜"
Inscribed verso: I. Cruikshanks [and in pencil]
A French Emigrant Cook
begging for a piece of English Roast Beef
Eyes where all the graces play,
all the Loves are met,
In Pity cease to turn away
From me ma Belle Coquette
Published: March 1, 1794, by Robert Sayer
Not in George; impression in WMC

A lean cook with his hair in a long queue kneels beseechingly beside a stout, ugly female cook, who grimaces at him. To the left there is a blazing hearth with pots; to the right, ovens.

22. THE OLD BATCHELOR ALARMED BY AN UNEXPECTED PRESENT

Pen and watercolor; 6½" x 6"
Inscribed verso: The Old Batchelor surprized / I. Cruikshanks
Published: May 12, 1794, by Laurie and Whittle
Not in George; impression in LWL

A baby in swaddling clothes lies on the ground in front of a door. An elderly man in a cap, holding a candle,

20. SMART SHOES MADE TO FIT—WITHOUT A LAST

comes out of the door followed by four other men; they look at the baby with dismay. A night watchman with a lantern stands to the left on the other side of the baby. In the background a young woman watches from around a corner. The street is named Providence Row.

23. THE KNOWING CROPS

Pen and watercolor; 7″ x 8⅝″
Inscribed verso: The Knowing Crops / I. Cruikshanks
Published: May 12, 179[4], by Laurie and Whittle; numbered 72
Not in George; impression in LWL

Two men, one thin, one stout, shake hands. They are dressed in the manner of the "bucks" of the period with very high-crowned hats, tight breeches, carrying clubs in their pockets.

On the print below the picture are the words:
Ha! Jack is it you–How are you dam-me

24. THE MERRY THOUGHT

Pen and monochrome gray wash; 6⅝″ x 9″
Inscribed verso: The Merry Thought / I. Cruikshanks
Published: May 12, 1794, by Laurie and Whittle; numbered 78
Not in George; impression in LWL

Three women and a man are seated around a table. The man has a wine glass in his hand; two of the women are about to break a wishbone. A Negro servant moves off to the left, eating from a plate he is carrying.

The impression of the plate in Mr. Lewis' collection does not contain any printed verses or other explanatory information concerning the scene, so the viewer is here to evolve his own interpretation.

25. CONCERT OF VOCAL & INSTRUMENTAL MUSIC, OR THE RISING GENERATION OF ORPHEUS

Pen and monochrome gray wash; 6½″ x 8⅜″
Inscribed verso: A Family Concert / I. Cruikshanks
Published: May 12, 1794, by Laurie and Whittle; numbered 84
Not in George; impression in LWL

A group of seven people are making music. An elderly woman plays a keyboard instrument, the music entitled "God Save the King." Beside this instrument sits a man playing a cello; behind the woman sits a man playing a violin; to the left (his back to us) a man plays a flute; the other figures are singing.

On the print eleven lines of verse concerning Orpheus are engraved below the title.

23. THE KNOWING CROPS

26. THE WEDDING

Pen and monochrome gray wash; 6¾" x 9⅜"
Inscribed verso: The Wedding / I. Cruikshanks
Published: May 12, 1794, by Laurie and Whittle; numbered 85
Not in George; impression in LWL

A young couple stand before a priest. The man places a ring on the woman's finger. Another young couple stand behind them; an elderly cleric (not in vestments) sits to the left with a book in his hand.

27. JUSTICE MITTIMUS AT A LOSS HOW TO ACT IN THIS AFFAIR

Pen and watercolor; 6⅞" x 10"
Inscribed verso: I really don't know your Worship–Some ill Natured P–has raised this report–If I have done any-thing amiss sir I am sure I was Dreaming–I. Cruikshanks
Published: May 12, 1794, by Laurie and Whittle
George 8575

A young girl stands before a justice seated in a high-back armchair. He has his hands folded and looks at the girl quizzically. Six other people are listening; to the left a man with an ear trumpet is seated, and another man is standing beside the justice's chair. To the right are three men and an old woman all seated; the woman titters behind her fan.

The following is engraved on the print:
My Dear little Girl what have you been about, they say you are pregnant–I really don't know your Worship–Some Wicked Wretch is the cause of this report –But if I have done any thing amiss Sir, I am sure I was Dreaming

28. SNOW BALLS—OR THE OLD BUCK IN DISTRESS

Pen and watercolor; 6¾" x 9½"
Inscribed verso: Snow Balls / I. Cruikshanks
Published: May 12, 1794, by Laurie and Whittle
George 8578

To the left two young women stand behind a tree, snowballs in their hands. A third kneels to make a snowball. They have been pelting a spindly, elderly man who walks to the right, fist clenched and cane raised. Three other figures are in the background to the right.

29. A SPOUTING CLUB

Pen and watercolor; 7" x 9⅝"
Inscribed verso: The Spouter / I. Cruikshanks
Published: May 12, 1794, by Laurie and Whittle
Not in George; impression in WMC

A man stands gesturing with great concern; his hat and a broken pipe lie on the floor near him. To the right

28. SNOW BALLS—OR THE OLD BUCK IN DISTRESS

four men sit at a counter, one holding a goblet and with a book open before him. To the left a man standing gestures with amazement and spills his tankard. In the background are two figures, one seated, the other declaiming from an open book.

Below the title on the print is engraved:
Is that a Dagger I see before me etc etc

30. A BOX-LOBBY CHALLENGE

Pen and watercolor; 6¾″ x 9″
Inscribed verso: A Box-Lobby Challenge / I. Cruikshanks
Published: May 12, 1794, by Laurie and Whittle
Not in George; impression in WMC

A man holding a club struts off to the right looking over his shoulder at another man, foppishly dressed, who eyes him through a quizzing glass. Three figures in the left background look on with amusement. The interior of a theater is visible to the right.

Below the title on the print is engraved:
Who are you Sir—Who am I—Phoo
All the world knows me Sir!—Damme who are you
Meet me tomorrow Morning in Hyde Park
I am Mr Plumb the Bankers fifteenth Clerk

31. GREAT PLENTY AND LITTLE WASTE

Pen and watercolor; 7″ x 8¾″
Inscribed verso: Great Plenty & no Waste / I. Cruikshanks
[also on the verso a pencil sketch of a duel]
Published: June 12, 1794, by Laurie and Whittle
George 8582

A plump young lady wears a dress with a low neckline and a very high waist. She carries a muff and walks toward a man in riding costume who inspects her through a quizzing glass. Behind her struts a stiff, short footman carrying a folded parasol. Two figures sit on a bench in the background.

32. THE FARMER'S RETURN—OR NEWS FROM LONDON

Pen and watercolor; 6⅞″ x 8⅞″
Signed: I C
Inscribed verso: The Farmer's return from London / I. Cruikshanks
Published: July 21, 1794, by Laurie and Whittle
George 8583

A well-dressed farmer sits on a chair, gesturing as he talks. To the left are three men and a woman. Two of the men are seated, and one spills a tankard of ale. To the right are a woman and five young children.

30. A BOX-LOBBY CHALLENGE

33. POOR SNIP AND FAMILY FRIGHTENED BY A THUNDER STORM

Pen and monochrome gray wash; 8⅜″ x 6⅞″
Inscribed verso: Poor Snip and Family in a Thunderstorm / I. Cruikshanks
Published: July 30, 179[4?], by Laurie and Whittle
Not in George; impression in WMC

Four figures in night clothes are huddled together with varying expressions of dismay. The woman to the left has a man's breeches around her neck. Lightning flashes outside the window to the right.

The style of the drawing suggests a date about 1790, a few years before it was actually published. The subject is contained in *Laurie & Whittle's Catalogue of New and Interesting Prints* (1795), p. 97, no. 67, where it is placed in the list with other prints known to have been issued in 1790 or 1791.

34. A CARD PARTY

Pen and watercolor; 6⅞″ x 8⅞″
Inscribed verso: A Whist Party / I. Cruikshanks
Published: August 16, 1794, by Laurie and Whittle
George 8584

Four elderly, ugly people sit around a card table, lighted with candles at the corners. A footman stands to the left holding a tray with two glasses; a man leans on the back of the chair of the card player to the right. Several figures are standing in the background.

35. THE DIFFICULT KISS

Pen and watercolor; 6⅞″ x 9¼″
Inscribed verso: A Difficult Kiss / I. Cruikshanks
[also another undecipherable inscription in a different hand]
Published: August 20, 1794, by Laurie and Whittle
Not in George; impression in LWL

A very stout man and woman attempt an embrace. Behind them is a counter with two tall decanters and a glass; there is a wing chair to the extreme right.

36. THE DANCING MASTER'S BALL

Pen and watercolor; 6⅞″ x 8¾″
Inscribed verso: The Dancing Masters' Ball / I. Cruikshanks
Published: August 27, 1794, by Laurie and Whittle; numbered 124
Not in George; impression in LWL

A man dances with a group of children; parents are seated, watching from the background. To the right are a fiddler and a man playing a wind instrument (recorder?).

36. THE DANCING MASTER'S BALL

37. THE FINISHING TOUCH

Pen and watercolor; 6⅝″ x 9¼″
Inscribed verso: The finishing Touch / I. Cruikshanks
Published: October 13, 1794, by Laurie and Whittle
George 8586

A young woman in a low-necked morning dress sits in a chair while a male hairdresser applies rouge to her cheek from a small box. To the left a servant pours a glass of wine; to the right is a dressing table with mirror and boxes. In Laurie and Whittle's list of prints (1795) the title is given as "The Finishing Touch of an Impure's Face."

38. ATTRACTION

Pen and watercolor; 7″ x 8⅞″
Inscribed verso: St. James' Park / I. Cruikshanks
Published: November 1, 1794, by Laurie and Whittle; numbered 129
Not in George; impression in LWL

Two men on the left, two women on the right walk all together, arms and hands linked. An old man with a cane watches them from the left, a young soldier from the right. Two other men are in the background.

On the print below the title is engraved:
Lovely Woman—There is in you all that We believe of Heaven

39. BLINDMAN'S BUFF

Pen and watercolor; 6¾″ x 9″
Inscribed verso: Blindman's Buff / I. Cruikshanks
[there are also several pen drawings of heads and figures on the verso]
Published: December 1, 1794, by Laurie and Whittle; numbered 131
Not in George; impression in LWL

A group of young people are playing blindman's buff. A boy, blindfolded, is about to be pushed by a girl over another girl kneeling on all fours. Two others entice him on. Another man and woman watch from the right background.

40. TIPPING ALL NINE

Pen and watercolor; 7⅛″ x 8¾″
Inscribed verso: Tipping all Nine / I. Cruikshanks
Published: December 1, 1794, by Laurie and Whittle; numbered 132
Not in George; impression in LWL

A group of men are playing and watching a game of nine pins. All nine have just fallen, but the leg of one spectator has been hit in the process. A woman looks on from behind a wooden fence.

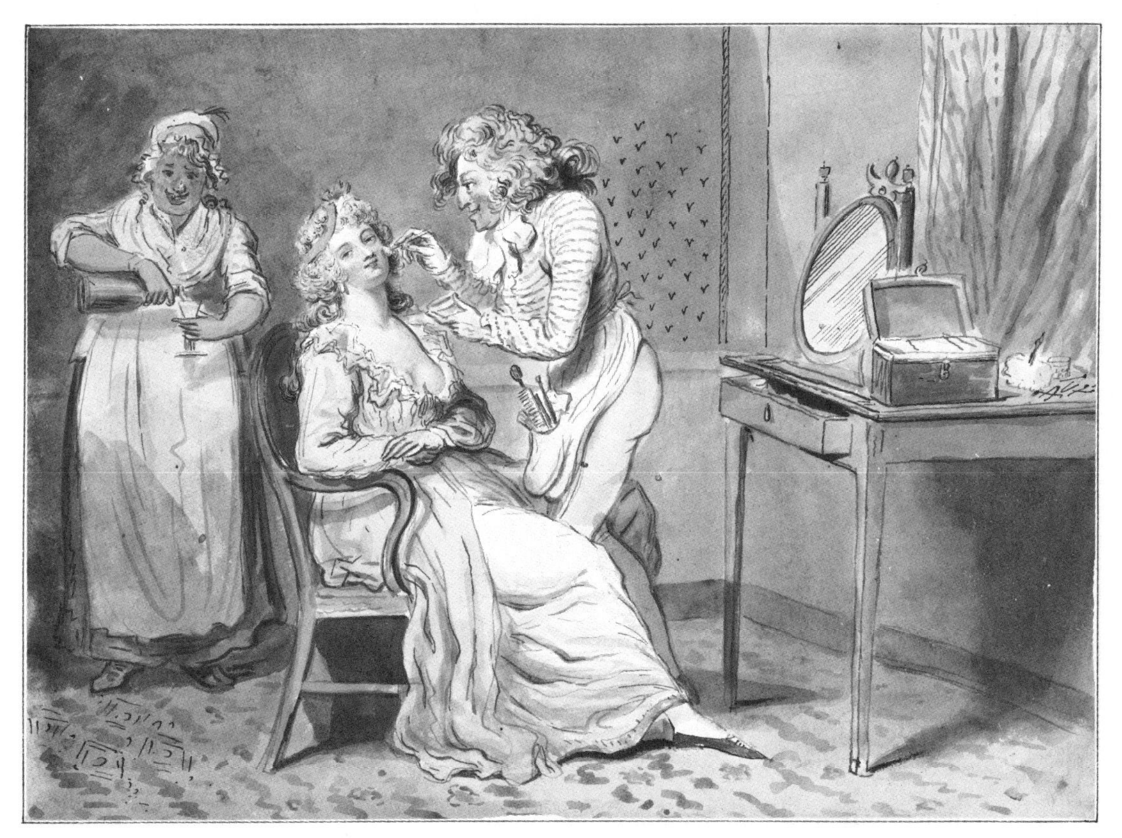

37. THE FINISHING TOUCH

41. DOCTORS DIFFER AND THEIR PATIENTS DIE

Pen and watercolor; 7″ x 9″
Inscribed verso: Doctors differ and their Patients Die / I. Cruikshanks
Published: December 24, 1794, by Laurie and Whittle; numbered 143
George 8590

Two doctors fight in the right foreground overturning a tripod table and spilling phials of medicine. To the left a patient, shrouded, sits in a high-back armchair.

42. FOGGY WEATHER

Pen and watercolor; 6⅝″ x 8¾″
Inscribed verso: Foggy Weather / I. Cruikshanks
Published: December 22, 1794, by Laurie and Whittle; numbered 144
George 8591

A stout cleric and a lady carrying a muff collide face to face; in the background left a man drives his horse into a pole; and, right, a man walks into a stream.

43. THE IRISH WEDDING

Pen and watercolor; 7″ x 8¾″
Inscribed verso: The Irish Wedding / I. Cruikshanks
No print after this design has been located; probably 1794

A dancing procession moves from right to left led by a diminutive fiddler. The bride and groom are second, followed by another dancing couple and an older dancing man. There is a church in the left background and a spectator waving at the procession.

A print entitled "Country Wedding" is included in *Laurie & Whittle's Catalogue of New and Interesting Prints* (1795), p. 98, no. 120. It is grouped with other prints issued in 1794.

44. A PAIR OF PRETTY ONES

Pen and watercolor; 6⅜″ x 9¼″
Inscribed verso: A pair of Pretty Ones / I. Cruikshanks
No print based on this drawing has been located; probably 1794

An aged and ugly old woman is seated in a high-back chair holding a fan in her left hand and an ear trumpet in her right, through which she listens to an equally old and ugly man who sits on her right. A younger man stands behind the chair of the speaker holding the top with his hands and observing the scene with amusement. There is a tripod table to the right with a decanter and one glass.

A print with this title appears in *Laurie & Whittle's Catalogue of New and Interesting Prints* (1795), p. 98, no. 125, following "Dancing Master's Ball," issued in 1794.

42. FOGGY WEATHER

45. LUCK IN THE LOTTERY

Pen and watercolor; 7″ x 8⅞″
Inscribed verso: Luck in the Lottery
No print based on this drawing has been located; probably 1794

A group of six men (one seated to left) exhibit great excitement and glee; one holds up a lottery ticket. To the right a woman stands holding a punch bowl. On the back wall is a picture labeled "A View of Bedlam."

A print with this title appears in *Laurie & Whittle's Catalogue of New and Interesting Prints* (1795), p. 98, no. 117, placed in the list along with other prints that appeared in 1794.

46. FOOT PAD'S—OR MUCH ADO ABOUT NOTHING

Pen and watercolor; 6½″ x 9⅜″
Inscribed verso: Gypsey Robbers / I. Cruikshanks
Published: May 4, 1795, by Laurie and Whittle
Not in George; impression in WMC

A well-built man stands terrified and drops his club at the sight of a blind, one-legged beggar who kneels behind a tombstone and aims his crutch like a gun. A Negro woman in tattered clothes lifts a pocket watch from the first man. Two other men flee in the background.

Below the print is engraved:
Buck's with Truncheons swagger and knock down
Insult the Sober Peasants when they're out of Town
But met by Lame Beggars, & a Mottley Crew
Their Courage fails them, & down they go.

47. DEBATING SOCIETY

Pen and watercolor; 6⅝″ x 9⅜″
Inscribed verso: The Debating Society / I. Cruikshanks
Published: May 5, 1795, by Laurie and Whittle; numbered 152
George 8771; impression with imprint intact WMC

A group of men debate, amplifying their remarks with gestures. The speaker on the rostrum, to left, calls for order with raised hammer. In the background a donkey brays through an open window. A sign on the back wall reads "Debate this Evening whether a mans wig should be Drest with Honey or Mustard." An inscription between the legs of the central figure reads "Thelwall." The reference is presumably to John Thelwall (1764-1834), reformer and lecturer on elocution, famed for his declamatory powers. Thelwall's name does not appear on the print. A tax on wig powder came into force on May 6, 1795; those wearing powder were to take out a guinea license (see under George 8629).

46. FOOT PAD'S—OR MUCH ADO ABOUT NOTHING

Beneath the title is engraved:
(Substitute for Hair Powder)
Silence Gentlemen! to Order! to Order, Only ten Speak at a time! for if you all Bray together, it's impossible to decide on this important Question.

48. CHARMS OF PRECEDENCE

Pen and watercolor; 7″ x 9″
Inscribed verso: Charms of Precedence / I. Cruikshanks
Published: August 7, 1795, by Laurie and Whittle; numbered 155
Not in George; impression in LWL

A disgruntled footman holds open a door while two dandies bow each other in. One has put his cane through a window; the other backs into a man, causing him to upset a tray full of food. There are eight lines of descriptive verse engraved below the print.

49. THE DISAGREEABLE INTRUSION, OR IRISH FORTUNE HUNTER DETECTED

Pen and watercolor; 6⅝″ x 9⅜″
Inscribed verso: The Fortune Hunter / I. Cruikshanks
Published: September 4, 1795, by Laurie and Whittle; numbered 160
Not in George; impression in LWL

A man in uniform kneels before an elderly woman who wears glasses and holds a fan. Another man with a club under his arm, holding a paper in his right hand, strides from the left toward the kneeling man. A third man, also holding a club, stands with arms crossed in the doorway to the left.

The following sentences appear on the print beneath the title:
On my knees Dear Lady let me intreat you to Appoint the happy Day—Pray Dear Sir rise it is too much for me to see you in such an humble situation. Bailiff—Pray rise and go along with us—We'll provide a Lodging for you—Murder—Thieves—Fire—Oh—Seize um Pomp-p-Oh-O-O

50. RAISING EVIL SPIRITS

Pen and watercolor; 6⅝″ x 9⅛″
Inscribed verso: The Fortune Teller / I. Cruikshanks
Published: November 20, 1795, by Laurie and Whittle; numbered 164
George 8777

A wizard is seated at a table to the right. He has a beard and wears very large spectacles. A snake coils around his left arm. With his right hand he holds a wand pointed at a circle in the floor from which emerge all manner of demons. Two frightened women stand within a circle to the left. A skull with tiny limbs moves along the floor from the right.

49. THE DISAGREEABLE INTRUSION, OR IRISH FORTUNE HUNTER DETECTED

51. SNAP DRAGON

Pen, gray and blue wash; 6¾″ x 9″
Inscribed verso: Snap Dragon / I. Cruikshanks [on the verso there is also a pencil sketch of a nude male figure]
Published: December 12, 1795, by Laurie and Whittle; numbered 165
George 8778

Six figures stand around a flaming bowl on a small round table. One man holds a terrified cat with its paw over the bowl. A man in the background gestures in an excited fashion with arms upraised. Snap dragon involved plucking raisins from flaming brandy.

52. MONSIEUR TONSON

Pen and watercolor; 6⅞″ x 8⅞″
Inscribed verso: Monsieur Tonson / I. Cruikshanks
Published: December 22, 1795, by Laurie and Whittle
Not in George; impression in WMC

Two young men stroll along a street arm in arm and pause to speak to a sleepy-looking man in ragged clothes who stands in an open doorway holding a candle. To the left a watchman sleeps in his box, his lighted lantern on the wall beside him. A man and woman converse in the right background.

There is a long story in verse engraved on the print concerning a man who for a joke continually calls at a particular house in the middle of the night asking for a Mr. Thomson.

53. THE PICKPOCKETS

Pen and watercolor; 6½″ x 9⅛″
Inscribed verso: I. Cruikshanks
No print based on this design has been located; ca. 1795

A street scene. A raggedly dressed boy bumps a torch against the knee of a stout cleric while another boy dives his hand into the cleric's pocket. Fashionably dressed figures are walking and conversing in the background.

54. COURTSHIP

Pen and watercolor; 6½″ x 8⅝″
Inscribed verso: Courtship / I. Cruikshanks
No print based on this drawing has been located; ca. 1795

A young man in riding clothes sits bolt upright with a startled look on his face. On the right a young woman leans forward on her chair and pats the man on the back. She has feathers in her hair and holds a fan in her left hand. On the left an old man sits in a high-back chair, his hands clasped over the top of a long walking stick.

51. SNAP DRAGON

55. LEADING APES IN HELL

Pen and watercolor; 6¾″ x 9⅛″
Inscribed verso: Leading Apes in Hell / I. Cruikshanks
No print after the drawing has been located; probably about 1795

Two ugly hags walk in the foreground, each holding leashes to which are attached several monkeys. Blue, tormenting demons stand on the shoulders and hair of the two hags. A third figure leads another group of monkeys in the background.

56. CLAIMING THE FLITCH OF BACON

Pen and watercolor; 6½″ x 9¼″
Inscribed verso: Claiming the Flitch of Bacon / I. Cruikshanks [also on verso, sketches of male figures in black and red pencil]
Published: February 8, 1796, by Laurie and Whittle; numbered 167
Not in George; impression in LWL

Two men on the right hold a side of bacon. A woman stands in the center holding open a large bag; a man beside her scratches his head. A stout man with a cane looks on amused from the left. Three figures are sketched in the right background.

Below the print is engraved:
Justice–Well, then you avou you have been Married Seven Years and never quarrell'd–If so you are entitled to the Flitch of Bacon, but I think that Bag is too small to hold it–Husband–So I told my Wife before we came from home and she has been abusing me like a Pickpocket ever since–an be rot' to her–Justice–Oh! ho, if that is the case–Here John hang up the Bacon again–lest she shou'd abuse you in carrying it home on account of its being too Heavy.

57. LOO

Pen and watercolor; 6¾″ x 9⅛″
Inscribed verso: Five Card Loo–Pam saves me / I. Cruikshanks
Published: February 20, 1796, by Laurie and Whittle, numbered 168
George 8922

Five people are seated around a table playing cards. A young woman to the right holds up five cards and looks smiling at the spectator. A man opposite her displays one card with pleasure. The other three players exhibit disappointment and distress.

Loo was a popular card game, played with four, five, six, or seven persons, preferably five or six. The Jack of Clubs is called "Pam" in the game and outranks all other cards. For a description of the game see *Hoyle's Improved Edition of the Rules for Playing*

56. CLAIMING THE FLITCH OF BACON

Fashionable Games at Cards (New York, 1830), pp. 138-153.

58. SOUND ARGUMENT—A DISPUTE BETWIXT WINE & WATER

Pen and watercolor; 6¾″ x 9¼″
Inscribed verso: Damit what are you about you are beating a Post—damme how should I know it was the Post. Why didn't he blow his Horn / I. Cruikshanks
Published: May 12, 1796, by Laurie and Whittle
Not in George; impression in WMC

A man bespattered and disheveled, his hat on the ground, stands arms akimbo in front of a pump. Two ladies look on with amusement from the left background.

Below the print is engraved:
You Rascal D-D-Demme. How dare you run against a Gemman—I suppose you mean to-to-to Rob me Curse you—but I'll take care of you-you-you Scoundrel. I'll have you sent on Bo-Board the Hulks ye Dog —Insult a Gemman hay-hay what do ye mean you Watery Rascal

59. THE ADVENTURES OF YOUNG WHIPSTITCH

Pen and watercolor; 6½″ x 8¾″
Inscribed verso: Adventures of Young Whipstitch / I. Cruikshanks
Published: August 12, 1796, by Laurie and Whittle
Not in George; impression in LWL

A group of six men are gathered around a table, all seated save one. The standing man (to the left) throws some coins on the table. A stout cleric tips the punch bowl to get the last of the punch. A young woman enters through a door to the right carrying another bowl of steaming punch.

There are verses on the engraving telling the story of a young man, the son of a tailor, who inherited a fortune from his father. The young man thought his father's trade beneath him and set off traveling to places where his background would not be known. Each place he visits, his hosts use some word or expression which he thinks reveals that they know his origin, although this is simply the result of his imagination and hypersensitivity.

60. MONSIEUR KANIFERSTANE: (OR, I DO NOT UNDERSTAND YOU.)

Pen and watercolor; 6½″ x 8⅝″
Inscribed verso: Monsieur Kaniferstain / I. Cruikshanks
Published: October 4, 1796, by Laurie and Whittle
Not in George; impression in LWL

An elegantly dressed Frenchman, hat in hand, speaks

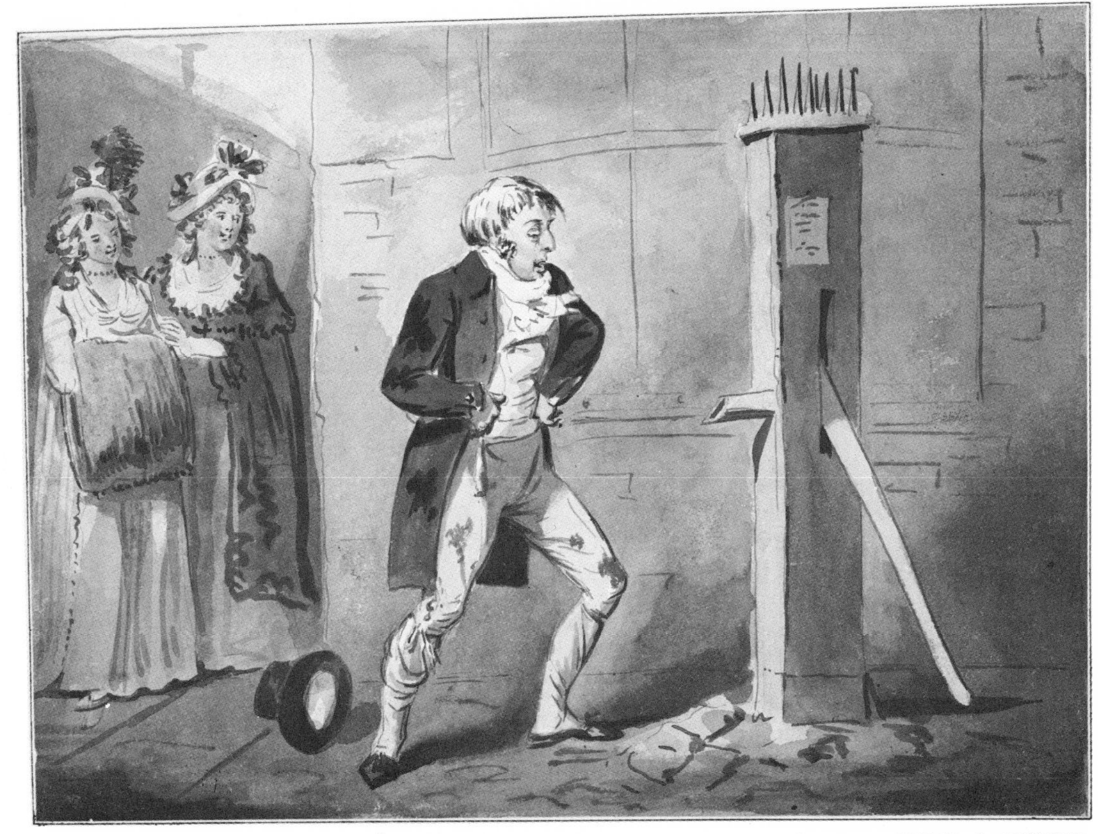

58. SOUND ARGUMENT—A DISPUTE BETWIXT WINE & WATER

to a stout Dutch burgher (in pantaloons) and his lady. Three Dutch children watch from behind and to the right. A boat is visible in the right background.

The verses on the print tell the story of a French marquis who visits Holland but does not know the language. When he inquires in French about the owner of a handsome palace, he receives the reply in Dutch "Ik kan niet verstaan," which he takes to mean Monsieur Kaniferstane. He receives the same answer when he inquires who is the husband of a pretty woman, and who is the winner of a large lottery. Finally he receives again the same reply when he inquires, while looking at a funeral cortege, who it is that has died.

61. WILL O' THE WISP, OR SOME FOLKES A LITTLE OUT OF THE ROAD

Pen and watercolor; 6⅜" x 9"
Inscribed verso: A Will o' the Wisp / I. Cruikshanks
Published: December 12, 1796, by Laurie and Whittle; numbered 177
Not in George; impression in LWL

An elderly couple have wandered in the dark into a bog, led on by a spritelike figure. A signpost is labeled "To the Devil." In the print the sign reads "The Road to Ruin." There are eight lines of descriptive verse on the print.

62. A VISIT TO THE BOARDING SCHOOL. THE GOVERNESS INTRODUCING LITTLE MISS TO PAPA AND MAMMA

Pen and watercolor; 6⅝" x 9⅛"
Inscribed verso: Charlotte at the Tomb of Werter / I. Cruikshanks
Published: June 20, 1797, by Laurie and Whittle; numbered 183
Not in George; impression in LWL

A stout, middle-aged couple stand to the left. The man has an umbrella under his arm; the woman, in a large hat and carrying a fan, is noticeably cross-eyed. To the right stand a young woman and a girl, the latter cross-eyed. Two children are seated at a desk in the right background. On the wall in the center is a picture of a woman beside a tomb inscribed "Werter."

Beneath the print is engraved:
Here Mrs. Parmesan is Charlotte at the Tomb of Werter, shall Miss Dorothy work that. Why I declare it looks wastly pretty I wow—Ah, and there's the Veeping-Villow, and all so natural, Well I'm sure—What think you of it Deary.—Why Love'e,—as for that there,—I have no objection in the Vorld,—against her Working Charlotte at the Tub of Water.

61. WILL O' THE WISP, OR SOME FOLKES A LITTLE OUT OF THE ROAD

63. LIGHT SUMMER TRAVELLING, ONLY SIX INSIDE, CHILDREN HALF PRICE

Pen and watercolor; 6⅝″ x 8½″
Inscribed verso: Plenty of Room Ma'am / I. Cruikshanks
Published: September 1, 1797, by Laurie and Whittle
George 9111

A stout lady, holding a fan and small dog, stands beside a coach, the door of which is being held open by the coachman who gestures inside, smiling. Five very fat men are visible inside the coach.

Beneath the title the following is engraved:
Just room for one Madam—Vell I wow I have run all the way like a Lamp-lighter, till I am all over in such a Heat you can't think.

64. THE DEAF JUSTICE

Pen and watercolor; 6⅝″ x 9⅛″
Inscribed verso: The Deaf Justice / I. Cruikshanks
Published: September 1, 1797, by Laurie and Whittle; numbered 197
Not in George; impression in LWL

An elderly man seated to the left behind a table, his foot on a gout stool, strains with hand to ear and mouth open to hear a man who stands before him on the other side of the table. A clerk sits at the back of the table; four other men (apparently laborers) stand to the right.

The following is engraved below the title on the print: Justice—Well Mr. Blunt, where was you at the time you discovered your Sheep—At Smithfield your Honor—At Smithfield very well, and what did you do there—I went to Handle'em you Worship—Handlum Handlum where's that, where do you say you went—I went to Handle'em an please your Honor. What have we to do with Handlum—I tell you fellow keep at Smithfield where you began your Story—and when we want you at Handlum we'll call upon you.

65. THE INSEPARABLE FRIENDS,—OR WEARY AFTER A WALK

Pen and watercolor; 7¼″ x 9¼″
Verso: There is a considerable amount of writing and a fragment of a pencil drawing. The writing is connected with Cruikshank's caricature "The Modern Leviathan" (George 8788), published by Fores on March 8, 1796. The drawing may be part of a discarded design for the same print. The name "I. Cruikshanks" is also inscribed on the verso, but there is no title given for the design on the front.
Published: September 8, 1797, by Laurie and Whittle; numbered 200
Not in George; impression in LWL

Two young women are sitting, apparently asleep, on a

63. LIGHT SUMMER TRAVELLING, ONLY SIX INSIDE, CHILDREN HALF PRICE

couch. The left wrist of one is joined to the right wrist of the other by a ribbon. Between them on the couch lies an open book entitled "Ovids Art of Love." A man standing behind the couch is about to tickle the nose of the lady on the right with a straw.

66. POOR PAT, OR A PRESENT OF WILD DUCKS

Pen and watercolor; 6¾" x 9⅛"
Inscribed verso: A present of a pair of Ducks / I. Cruikshanks
Published: September 25, 1797, by Laurie and Whittle; numbered 201
Not in George; impression in LWL

A servant stands to the left, an open basket at his feet. He speaks to a middle-aged man who sits at a table holding a letter with his left hand. A younger woman is seated behind the table, and a child stands beside her.

Below the title the following is engraved on the print:
Why Pat, I find here in the Letter, a Brace of live Wild Ducks your Master has sent me

Pat. In the Letter, . . . is it the Letter you say,—By Jesus, I'm glad you found 'em there, for they flew all out of the Basket while I was Drinking a Noggin of Whiskey with Murphy O'Flanegan,—Oh! Botheration,—good luck to me—hurra—hurra Oh!—Your Sarvant Sir

67. A MATRIMONIAL PUZZLE

Pen and watercolor; 6¾" x 9¼"
Inscribed verso: Mr. Do-Nothing / I. Cruikshanks
Published: October 10, 1797, by Laurie and Whittle; numbered 202
George 9838 (undated); impression with imprint intact in LWL

A man and a woman sit on either side of a small, square table. The man, smoking a pipe, leans forward on his chair, his elbows on the table. The lady, facing the spectator, has her arms folded and her feet crossed. A young man enters the room by a door at the left.

The following is engraved below the title:
Husband—What makes you look so thoughtful my Love, what are you puzzling your Dear Head about now

Wife—Why you said last Night at Supper, that you knew every one in our Street were Cuckolds but one—And I have been Puzzling Myself ever since to find out who that one could be

Husband—Oh! Oh! Very well, I have done.

66. POOR PAT, OR A PRESENT OF WILD DUCKS

68. A SCOTCH REEL

Pen and watercolor; 7″ x 9⅞″
Inscribed verso: St. Andrews Day / I. Cruikshanks
Published: by Laurie and Whittle, the date not clear, possibly 1797
Not in George; impression in WMC

Two couples, the men wearing kilts, do a lively Scottish dance. A man seated in the right foreground plays the bagpipes. In the left background is a building with the sign "Whiskey" above the door.

69. THE OLD CHEESE

Pen and watercolor; 6¾″ x 9″
Inscribed verso: The Old Cheese / I. Cruikshanks
Published: February 1, 1798, by Laurie and Whittle
George 9332

A man stands at the head of a table around which sit seven other people. He holds a cheese between his two hands; other cheeses fly about the room.

The print bears the subtitle:
An Original Tale, recited by Mr. Fawcett, at Covent-Garden Theater.

The verses, in two columns, tell the story of a farmer who tries to impress his guests with his domestic authority but is eventually quelled by his wife.

70. A BONE TO PICK

Pen and watercolor; 6¾″ x 9⅛″
Inscribed verso: A Bone to Pick / I. Cruikshanks
Published: February 1, 1798, by Laurie and Whittle
Not in George; impression in WMC

A family (a man, his wife, and four children) sit around a dinner table. The man, to the left, is gorging himself. His wig is on the chair behind him, a tankard of ale on the floor beside him; what appear to be two horns are sprouting from his head. Three of the children are eating at the table; the mother (who sits opposite her husband) is nursing the fourth. A picture on the wall is labeled "Horn Fair."

Beneath the title on the print is engraved:
Wife–I'll thank you for a bit more meat. Husband–No I think you've had enough but there's a Bone for you and be contented

Wife–Very well as this is always the case–I'll give you a Bone to Pick that's got Flesh on it–There's the four Children at the Table, and only one of them is Yours–now Pick that one out and be Contented

71. MORE, STRANGE, AND WRIGHT

Pen and watercolor; 6⅝″ x 9⅛″
Inscribed verso: Messrs. Moor Strange & Wright / I. Cruikshanks

68. A SCOTCH REEL

Published: February 12, 1798, by Laurie and Whittle; numbered 208
Not in George; impression in LWL

Three men in jovial humor are seated around a small table with a bowl of punch, glasses, and a lighted candle. Two of the men smoke long pipes; two dogs are on the floor to the right.

Beneath the title on the print is engraved:
At a Tavern one Night
Messrs More, Strange, and Wright;
Met to Drink, and good thoughts to Exchange:
Says More, of us three,
The whole Town will agree:
There's only one Knave and thats Strange.
Yes says Strange rather sore,
I'm sure there's one More;
A most terrible knave and a bite:
Who cheated his Mother,
His Sister, his Brother;
O yes replied More, that is Wright

72. FRANK HAYMAN; A TALE

Pen and watercolor; 6⅝″ x 9⅜″
Inscribed verso: Frank Hayman and the Hare / I. Cruikshanks
Published: February 20, 1798, by Laurie and Whittle
George 9333

A porter in an apron offers a mangled hare to a startled maidservant standing to the left in an open door marked "Hayman." To the right, behind the porter, stands a man in a black hat, holding a cane in his right hand, gesturing with his left index finger.

The engraving is on a sheet with forty verses, described as:
Written by John Taylor, Esquire, Author of Monsieur Tonson, and originally intended for recitation at the Haymarket Theatre, during the Lent season.

The verses relate a story about the painter Francis Hayman (1708-1776), who followed with amusement a drunken porter delivering a hare. While the porter dozed, a dog ate part of the hare. Hayman expected an entertaining scene when the porter arrived at his destination but discovered instead that he was the victim of his own sense of humor, for the hare was intended for the painter himself.

Isaak Cruikshank's son George treated this same subject in Plate 34 to *The Humorist*, 1819 (George William Read, *The Works of George Cruikshank* [London, 1871], Vol. I, no. 823).

72. FRANK HAYMAN; A TALE

73. THE DOCTOR SNATCHING AT THE GUINEA AFTER HIS PATIENT IS DEAD

Pen and watercolor; 6⅝″ x 9⅛″
Inscribed verso: The Last Fee / I. Cruikshanks
Published: March 6, 1798, by Laurie and Whittle; number not clear, probably 209
Not in George; impression in LWL

A doctor rushes forward to seize a coin from the hand of his patient who has just died. A manservant and a maid restrain him.

Beneath the title on the print is engraved:
Oh let me die in peace! Eumenes cried,
To a hard Creditor at his bed-side;
How! die! roar'd Gripus, and thus your Debts evade:
By God, Sir, you shan't die till I am paid.
Also: Vide Philosophical Transactions of T. Schamburgh

74. THE HONEST TARS AND MARINES OF THE ARGONAUT

Pen and watercolor; 6⅝″ x 9″
Inscribed verso: Sailors Contribution / I. Cruikshanks
Published: March 12, 1798, by Laurie and Whittle; numbered 210
George 9185

A group of sailors crowd around a large wooden tub, bottom up, on which they are tossing coins. To the left a sailor, with GR tattooed on his arm, reaches deep in his pocket; an officer behind the tub opens his purse; to the right a sailor with a large tankard extends his hand to an army (?) officer. Signs attached to the mast in the background read "God save the King," "Rule Britannia."

On the print the following is engraved beneath the title:
Contributing Nobly against the Enemies of Old England with the Original Letter Addressed to their Commander Lieutenant P. Hue "Argonaut, Jany 31st 1798 / Sir, / We the Seamen and Marines of his Majesty's Ship Argonaut, under your command, desire to give 10s each man out of our wages, to drive before us into the sea all French / scoundrels, and other blackguards that would take their parts / We are / Your faithful servants / John Mitchell, Boatswain's Mate, for Self and Ships Company / Alex. Hean, Sergeant for Self and Party / God save the King."

75. MONMOUTH STREET MUTTON

Pen and watercolor; 6⅝″ x 9″
Inscribed verso: Monmouth Street Mutton / I. Cruikshanks
Published: March 16, 1798, by Laurie and Whittle; numbered 211
Not in George; impression in LWL

74. THE HONEST TARS AND MARINES OF THE ARGONAUT

Three men stand in front of a butcher's stall; the one to the left has his arms folded; the man in the center reaches for a leg of mutton hung on a rack; the man to the right sharpens a knife. A woman stands in a door in the background; two men converse in the right background. A sign on a building reads "Monmouth Street"; another sign reads "Second hand Cloath."

Beneath the title on the print is engraved:
Pat—Hurra Measter, and what do ye Ax for this here Shoulder of Mutton

Butcher—Why that there leg of Mutton, will be four and six pence. I cut it from as nice a Ship as any in Smithfield

Pat—Oh botheration, who do ye take me for, blarneying me over, wid your Ship, and your Second hand Mutton, I can buy a New one in Fleet-Market for half that—So good Morning to you Honor, as the Devil said to the Pope.

76. PADDY AND THE FIREMAN

Pen and watercolor; 8¼″ x 6⅝″
Inscribed verso: House on Fire / I'm only a Lodger / I. Cruikshanks
Published: March 16, 1798, by Laurie and Whittle; numbered 212
Not in George; impression in LWL

A helmeted fireman holding a hatchet and torch calls to a startled man in bed; a dog, barking from beneath the bed, has upset a chamber pot.

Beneath the title on the print is engraved the following:

Fire Man—Get up my Friend, get up directly, the House is on Fire.

Irish Man—Botheration seize you and the House both, I have no business at all, at all with it, I'm only a Lodger.

77. RINGING THE CHANGES—OR QUIZZING MY UNCLE

Pen and watercolor; 6⅝″ x 9⅛″
Inscribed verso: The Spendthrift I. Cruikshanks
Published: March 20, 1798, by Laurie and Whittle; numbered 213
George 9323

An old man and a young man are seated at a table with decanter and glasses. The old man, to the left, holds a newspaper; the young man, with hat and cane, gestures toward his companion.

A secondary title engraved on the plate is:
Old Nunke and his Hopeful Nephew.

77. RINGING THE CHANGES—OR QUIZZING MY UNCLE

Below the engraving there is the following explanation:

Old Gentleman (Reading) Last Monday A Society of College Youths Rang a Peal of 4000, 500 Changes in the Space of two Hours and twenty-Minutes, upon a Set of Treble-bob Majors, being the Shortest time ever known, what do you think of that Jack. Nephew—Mere nothing Uncle—I ring the Changes to the Tune of more than double that Sum in Half the time, on two Generals, and one Simple-Colonel—will you lend me a Hundred Pound for two or three days Uncle.

78. CAPTAIN WATTLE AND MISS ROE

Pen and watercolor; 5⅞″ x 8½″
Inscribed verso: Capt. Whattle & Miss Roe / I. Cruikshanks
Published: April 4, 1798, by Laurie and Whittle; numbered 214
George 9324

A one-eyed woman holding a decanter and a peg-legged naval officer are having a scrap. Four figures watch with amusement from the other side of a table. A man enters by a door on the right up which a cat has climbed. A small dog cavorts in the foreground.

79. THE NATURALIST'S VISIT TO THE FLORIST

Pen and watercolor; 6⅞″ x 9″
Inscribed verso: "Marocco's Emperor by the livin God" / Vide, Peter Pindar / I. Cruikshanks
Published: May 24, 1798, by Laurie and Whittle; numbered 218
George 9326

A fat man tramples a bed of flowers in an attempt to catch a butterfly in his wig. Another fat man gestures in dismay. He sits in a bathchair being pushed by a male servant.

Beneath the title is engraved:

A Gentleman who was remarkably fond of raising fine Tulips, shewing his Collection to a Friend who was equally curious in Butterflies, a scarce Fly called the Emperor of Morocco presenting itself to our Naturalist . . . He without any hesitation made his way over the whole Bed to seize the prize . . .

Peter Pindar, in *Sir Joseph Banks and the Emperor of Morocco*, 1788, describes Banks as chasing this butterfly.

80. BILLING AND COOING AT THE JELLY SHOP

Pen and watercolor; 6¾″ x 8⅞″
Inscribed verso: Eating Ice / I. Cruikshanks

80. BILLING AND COOING AT THE JELLY SHOP

Published: June 4, 1798, by Laurie and Whittle; numbered 219
George 9327

A man and woman are seated in front of a counter. The woman, with her arms folded, is being fed a spoonful of jelly by the man. A second man, to the right, leaning on the counter, ogles the pair through his glass. His reflection appears in a large oval mirror on the wall. A waitress watches from the right background.

The plate gives no further indication of any story or anecdote involved.

81. THE GRACES COMPARING SANDALS

Pen and watercolor; 8¾″ x 6⅝″
Inscribed verso: The Graces comparing Sandals / I. Cruikshanks
Published: July 4, 1798, by Laurie and Whittle; numbered 220
George 9328

Three fashionably dressed young women, two standing and one seated, are in a boudoir. The two standing lift their skirts to reveal their ankles. On the wall behind is a picture of the Judgment of Paris.

82. HELTER SKELTER—OR A SHOWER ON GREENWICH HILL

Pen and watercolor; 6⅝″ x 9⅛″
Signed: Cruikshank 1798
Inscribed verso: Shower of Rain on Greenwich Hill / I. Cruikshanks
Published: August 20, 1798, by Laurie and Whittle; numbered 221
George 9329

A group of people run from left to right down a slope during a shower. In the center a young man holds an umbrella over a young woman; to the left a fat man has fallen on his back.

83. ENJOYING A FRIEND

Pen and watercolor; 6¾″ x 9″
Signed: Cruikshank 179[?] [both the name and date have been clipped]
Inscribed verso: Smoking Companions / I. Cruikshanks
Published: August 21, 1798, by Laurie and Whittle; numbered 222
George 9330

Two men, looking gloomy, sit on either side of a small square table smoking long pipes. On the table are a large frothing tankard and a paper. Sixteen lines of verse are engraved beneath the design.

82. HELTER SKELTER—OR A SHOWER ON GREENWICH HILL

84. SPECULATION: OR, A NEW WAY OF SAVING A THOUSAND POUNDS

Pen and watercolor; 6½″ x 9″
Signed and dated: Cruikshank 179 [the last digit is clipped and not decipherable]
Published: October 12, 1798, by Laurie and Whittle
Not in George; impression in LWL

Two men are seated at a table with decanter and glasses; one man, his hands on the table, has partially risen, an expression of indignation on his face. The other man, smiling, points behind him to the right at a young woman standing in front of a window. A groom, also smiling, stands behind the first man. Prominent in the background is a picture with a recumbent figure in armor from whom issues a genealogical tree.

The print is accompanied by 138 lines of verse relating the story of an impoverished gambler who wangles a dinner with a promise to tell his host how he can save £1,000. After discovering that his host has a handsome daughter of marriageable age with a dowry of £10,000, the gambler offers (as his device for saving £1,000) to marry the daughter for £9,000.

85. PATIENCE; OR, A BAD JOB

Pen and watercolor; 6⅜″ x 9″
Inscribed verso: I. Cruikshanks
Published: November 20, 1798, by Laurie and Whittle
George 9335

A stout clergyman, his back to the fire, gestures in rage at a servant who drops a jug as he runs to the right from the room. A lady seated to the left restrains the clergyman by catching his coattail.

The print is subtitled:
An original tale. Written by the Author of Speculation.

Mrs. George suggests that the reference is to C. Anstey, *Speculation; or a Defence of Mankind*, but the poem on the print does not appear in the collected edition of Anstey's works brought out by his son.

The poem relates a story of a parson who, after giving a sermon on the misfortunes and patience of Job, falls into a rage when a servant announces that the contents of a cask of ale has been spilled.

86. IRISH METHOD OF CURING A SMOKEY CHIMNEY

Pen and watercolor; 6⅝″ x 9″
Inscribed verso: The Smoaky Chimney / I. Cruikshanks
Published: December 18, 1798, by Laurie and Whittle; numbered 223
Not in George; impression in LWL

A man sits tumbled on the floor in front of a smoking

84. SPECULATION: OR, A NEW WAY OF SAVING A THOUSAND POUNDS

fireplace. Behind him a servant with a malicious grin tips two chairs and a table. A third man, hands raised, stands in a doorway to the left.

The verses under the print relate a story about cleaning a blocked chimney by throwing a brick down it from the roof.

87. THE PARSON COME HOME RATHER GROGGY

Pen and watercolor; 6¼″ x 8⅞″
Signed: Cruikshanks 1798
No print based on this drawing has been located.

A stout parson is seated backward on his horse, which has stopped at the door to the stable. To the right the parson's wife, carrying a lamp, comes forward from the door of the house. Two other figures look on with amusement from the interior of the house.

88. DRINK TO ME ONLY WITH THINE EYES

Pen and watercolor; 6⅞″ x 9″
Inscribed verso: "Drink to me only with thine eyes" / I. Cruikshanks
Published: January 4, 1799, by Laurie and Whittle; numbered 224
George 9494

A middle-aged couple sit on either side of a small square table; each holds a glass of wine, and they smile at each other. There is a decanter on the table; an oval picture of Cupid on the wall is labeled "Beware."

On the print eight lines of the song by Ben Jonson are engraved beneath the design.

89. A COLD SEASON

Pen and watercolor; 6¾″ x 8⅞″
Inscribed verso: Snowy weather in London
Published: February 12, 1799 (bearing I. Cruikshanks' name as artist), by Laurie and Whittle; numbered 227
George 9496; dated impression in WMC

A street scene in snow. Two women walk forward holding large muffs to their faces. In the left foreground a boy has slipped, spilling a tray of food he was carrying. An old man leaves a lottery office carrying a blank ticket. Other figures walk on the street bundled against the cold. In the background two men shovel snow from a roof.

90. TRUE BLUE

Pen and watercolor; 7⅛″ x 8⅞″
Inscribed verso: All alive at Portsmouth / I. Cruikshanks
Published: April 4, 1799, by Laurie and Whittle; numbered 228
George 9497

A coach, overflowing with sailors and young women, moves from left to right pulled by two horses. A man

89. A COLD SEASON

holding a bottle rides backward on one of the horses; another man standing on top of the coach plays a fiddle.

On the print beneath the title is engraved:

The Jolly Tars of Old England or all alive at Portsmouth

91. ENGLISH IMPROVEMENTS ON FRENCH FASHIONS

Pen and watercolor; 6⅞″ x 8¾″
Inscribed verso: A Frenchmans Story / I. Cruikshanks
Published: April 8, 1799, by Laurie and Whittle; numbered 230
Not in George; impression in LWL

Four men sit about a small round table on which are a decanter and glasses as well as a coffee pot and cup and saucer. The man to the right, very thin, is dressed in the French manner with elaborate ruffs and a sword. The man to the left is stout and has his hands on his chest. The two men behind listen to the Frenchman.

Beneath the print is engraved:

Frenchman—Begar My Country be ver clever in de invention of de Fashions—dis is one, de ruffle—it be one grand ornament to de hand.

Englishman—Certainly it is a great ornament to the hand, but according to custom my Country has made great improvement upon that Invention, by adding a Shirt to it.

92. NEHEMIAH'S DISASTER—A TALE

Pen and watercolor; 6⅝″ x 9″
Inscribed verso: Nehemiah's Disaster / I. Cruikshanks
Published: April 9, 1799, by Laurie and Whittle; numbered 229
George 9498

A woman sits up in bed holding a crying baby. A man walks from right to left holding a taper in his right hand and a child's commode in his left.

On the print the incident is related in biblical language:

And behold about the ninth hour Tabitha the Wife of my Bosom awoke, . . . [etc.].

93. ROBIN & SUE

Pen and watercolor; 6¼″ x 9⅛″
Signed: Cruikshanks 1799
Inscribed verso: Raising Recruits / I. Cruikshanks
Published: April 12, 1799, by Laurie and Whittle; numbered 231
Not in George; impression in LWL

A soldier and a young countryman stand together, their left hands clasped. The countryman holds a bowl

91. ENGLISH IMPROVEMENTS ON FRENCH FASHIONS

in his right hand; the soldier has his right hand above the yokel's head, first and last fingers extended to look like horns. To the right in front of a cottage is a woman holding a baby; another soldier and a man are standing in the doorway. To the left, two boys in military dress play fife and drum.

Beneath the title on the print is engraved:
I'll list for a Soldier!—said Robin to Sue,

To avoid those eternal disputes:
Ay, ay—cried the termagant—do Robin do,
Mean time—I'll be Raising Recruits.

94. UNRULY PIGS

Pen and watercolor; 6¾″ x 9″
Signed: Cruikshanks 1799
Inscribed verso: Unruly Pigs / I. Cruikshanks
Published: May 20, 1799, by Laurie and Whittle; numbered 232
Not in George; impression in LWL

A herd of pigs run pell-mell through a crowded street creating havoc everywhere. A wheelbarrow full of fruit is upset; a ladder with a man on it falls to the ground; a haberdashery shop is in confusion; a stout man falls on his back in the left foreground.

95. ROBIN AND HIS HORSE

Pen and watercolor; 6⅝″ x 8⅞″
Signed: Cruikshank 1799
Inscribed verso: Robin, of the Temple of the M . . . s / and his Horse Apollo / I. Cruikshanks
No print after the drawing has been located.

A night scene, the moon in the upper left corner. A man who has fallen from his horse looks at the animal, which also turns its head to look at the man. A signpost in the background is inscribed "To Broxbourn by Enfield."

The draftsmanship as well as the color in this drawing are unusually crude for Cruikshank, but this is not one of the drawings singled out by George Cruikshank as not by his father.

96. PADDY WHACK'S FIRST RIDE IN A SEDAN

Pen and watercolor; 7⅜″ x 9¼″
Inscribed verso: Irish Chairmen / I. Cruikshanks
Published: January 28, 1800, by Laurie and Whittle; numbered 238
Not in George; impression in LWL

Two jovial chairmen carry a sedan. The passenger (whose feet are visible below the sedan and whose

96. PADDY WHACK'S FIRST RIDE IN A SEDAN

hand protrudes through the top) is in obvious discomfort. A man carrying a basket on his head watches with amusement from the left.

Below the title on the print is engraved:
Arrah! my dear Honey—to be sure I'd rather walk, if it wasn't for the Fashion of the thing.

97. THE OLD DOG'S LEGACY

Pen and watercolor; 7⅛" x 9"
Inscribed verso: Fee for Burying a Dog in the Ch. Yard / I. Cruikshanks
Published: February 1, 1800, by Laurie and Whittle; numbered 239
Not in George; impression in LWL

A jolly, stout clergyman stands with his back to a fireplace. He puts out his left hand to receive some coins from a man dressed in riding clothes; there is a dog behind the second man. A clerk watches from a high desk to the left. A church is visible through a window to the right.

Beneath the print is engraved:
Vicar: How could you be so profane as to Inter your Dog in the Church Yard, You are liable to be punished in the Spiritual Court.

Farmer: Why aye Doctor, but when you consider what a sensible creature he was, you will not be so severe, the day before he died he made his Will and left you a Legacy.

Vicar: a Legacy

Farmer: Yes he left you 6 Guineas, & I'se come to give it to you

Parson: Oho if that's the case why did you not mention it before, & he might have laid inside the Church.

98. LEAP YEAR—OR LOVE IN PLENTY

Pen and watercolor; 6¾" x 9⅜"
Inscribed verso: Leap Year / I. Cruikshanks
Published: March 18, 1800, by Laurie and Whittle; numbered 241
Not in George; impression in LWL

Two young women hold a young man; a third woman hurries toward them with outstretched arms. In the left and right background are two groups each with an older man pursued by a woman.

99. ST. ANDREW'S DAY

Pen and watercolor; 7⅛" x 9¼"
Inscribed verso: St. Andrews Day / I. Cruikshanks
Published: November 1, 1800, by Laurie and Whittle
Not in George; impression in WMC

A group of Scottish country folk are gathered around

97. THE OLD DOG'S LEGACY

a table. A woman pierces the haggis with a knife and the contents spurt into the face of a man seated to the left. In the center background a solemn-looking man raises his hands in prayer. To the left a young girl carries in a black ram's head on a platter. A couple dances in a room in the right background.

100. IRISH FORTUNE HUNTER

Pen and watercolor; 6⅝″ x 9⅛″
Inscribed verso: Irish Fortune Hunter / I. Cruikshanks
No print based on this drawing has been located; ca. 1800

A man rather elaborately dressed and wearing a large hat stands in the center of a room, a cane in one hand, a glass of wine in the other. To the left is a servant holding a tray and decanter. In the right background are two women, one seated on a sofa, apparently drying her eyes.

101. THE POOR POET

Pen and watercolor; 6¾″ x 8¾″
Inscribed verso: The poor Poet / I. Cruikshanks
No print based on this drawing has been located; ca. 1800

A very thin man, out at the elbows, sits in front of a fireplace smoking a pipe and holding a tankard. He rests his arm on a small square table on which are a lighted candle, some papers, and other objects. In the left background is a bed with a woman and three children asleep. Two of the children have their heads at the foot of the bed.

102. THE SENSES

Pen and watercolor; 7″ x 9⅜″
Inscribed verso: The Senses / I. Cruikshanks
No print based on this drawing has been located; probably ca. 1800

A young couple sitting on a sofa embrace and kiss; the woman holds a flower under the nose of a young child and also steps on the tail of a cat. An old man, fists clenched, watches the scene through a hole in the door. A servant stands behind him, his finger to his nose.

103. THE FAMILY PHYSICIAN

Pen and watercolor; 7″ x 9″
Inscribed verso: Too Good Health / I. Cruikshanks
Published: January 20, 1801, by Laurie and Whittle; numbered 256
Not in George; impression in LWL

A very plump, rosy-cheeked man sits in a high-back chair. A physician seated to the right feels the pulse of the first man. In the left background a woman holds a pot over a fire in a fireplace.

100. IRISH FORTUNE HUNTER

Beneath the print is engraved:
Oh! my dear Doctor I am very bad—I do not know what is the matter with me—I eat well, drink well—and I sleep well— Doctor—Ah! Dreadful symptoms indeed—Well well I'll give you something that shall take away all that.

104. THE WELCH TRAVELLER

Pen and watercolor; 6⅞" x 9"
Inscribed verso: The Welsh Ambassador / I. Cruikshanks
Published: February 4, 1801, by Laurie and Whittle; numbered 258
Not in George; impression in LWL

A man mounted on a Welsh pony, a leek in his hat, knocks with his stick at the door of an inn called "Packhorse." The innkeeper's head appears in an opening beside the door.

Under the print is engraved:
Open the Door directly Landlord, to Shon ap Morgan —ap Shenkin—ap Jones—ap Thomas—ap Williams—ap Evans—ap Griffith—ap Owen—ap Rice—ap Morris; Shentleman of Wales—I will not open the Door, there is so many of you, my little Inn won't contain one half of you.

105. FELLOW FEELING

Pen and watercolor; 7" x 9"
Inscribed verso: The awkward Servant / I. Cruikshanks
Published: February 4, 1801, by Laurie and Whittle; numbered 259
Not in George; impression in LWL

A servant, to the left, who has been bitten on the leg by a small dog, spills a tea tray. Two women to the right, one seated and one standing, look and gesture in surprise.

Below the title is engraved:
Good lack a day John, what are you doing? you have broke all the tea things. I can't help it Ma'am, that nasty cur of yours has bit my leg. Bit your leg! has he? dear me; I hope the pretty little creature won't be sick after it!!

106. AN INNKEEPER'S DAUGHTER SHEWING TOWN BUCKS TO THEIR CHAMBER

Pen and watercolor; 6½" x 8¾"
Inscribed verso: Lodgings to Let / I. Cruikshanks [also verso a full-length pencil sketch of a young woman pulling up a stocking]
Published: April 20, 1801, by Laurie and Whittle
Not in George; impression in WMC

A young man ogles a young woman and holds her

106. AN INNKEEPER'S DAUGHTER SHEWING TOWN BUCKS TO THEIR CHAMBER

right hand; she has a bundle of keys in her left hand. A second young man, to the left, examines the lady through his eyeglass. A dog and cat spat in the background. A window to the right has the sign (the lettering in reverse) "Lodgings / furnished."

On the print below the picture is engraved:
Here Gentlemen is a two bedded Room, or you may have seperate Rooms. The Beds are well aired I assure you–Can I have you as a companion my Love? Oh no Sir But you may have my Cat–Tibby

107. THE UNLUCKY SHOWER—LONDON LADIES GOING TO A COUNTRY DANCE

Pen and watercolor; 6¼" x 9⅜"
Inscribed verso: London Ladies going to a Country Dance / I. Cruikshanks
Published: May 1, 1801, by Laurie and Whittle; numbered 263
George 9837

An open wagon, labeled "Common Stage," contains four ladies standing, wrapped in blankets to protect themselves from the rain. The wagon, moving from right to left, is drawn by two horses with two well-dressed young men acting as driver and leader.

108. ST. DAVID'S DAY

Pen and watercolor; 7¼" x 9½"
Inscribed: St. Davids Day. I. Cruikshanks
Published: May 1, 1801, by Laurie and Whittle (the engraving is the reverse of the drawing)
Not in George; impression in WMC

A short, stout man carrying a hat with a leek on it dances with a young woman. To the right a seated man plays some sort of mouth instrument. A man in the background holds up a cheese and a bundle of leeks. To the left four men sit or stand in front of a large open hearth on which kettles are cooking. All the figures wear leeks in their hats.

109. LITTLE MOUTHS

Pen and watercolor; 6⅜" x 9¼"
Inscribed verso: Little Mouths / I. Cruikshanks
Published: May 25, 1801, by Laurie and Whittle; numbered 265
Not in George; impression in LWL

Three men and two women are gathered outside the door of an inn. One woman, arms crossed, has her mouth open at full stretch. A countryman, to the left, looks on smiling, holding a tankard in one hand and a long horsewhip in the other. Two other men, one

108. ST. DAVID'S DAY

standing in the door, the other seated at a table, are to the right. A covered cart is in the left background.

Below the print is engraved:
Betty with bridled chin extends her face
And then contracts her lips with simp'ring grace,
Cry'd, hem! pray what must all the huge ones do
For husbands, when we little mouths have two?
Hold, not so fast, cry'd he, pray pardon me,
Maids with huge gaping wide mouths must have three,
Betty distorts her face with hideous squall,
And mouth of a foot wide began to bawl.
Oh! ho! is't so? the case is alter'd Paul,
Is that the point? I wish the three were ten,
I warrant I'll find Mouth if they'll find Men

110. THE WIG AND THE WAGS

Pen and watercolor; 6¾" x 9⅛"
Inscribed verso: Having lost your Hat, I beg leave to take your Wig
Published: June 24, 1801, by Laurie and Whittle
Not in George; impression in WMC

A man lifts a wig from the head of a stout elderly man who supports himself on a cane and a hitching post. Another man carrying a hat disappears around the corner of a building. The tower of St. George's Bloomsbury is visible in the distance.

In the print two women are added to the left. Below the print is engraved:
Follow the thief replied the stander by
Ah Sir said he, these feet will wag no more
Alarm the neighborhood with hue and cry
Alas! I've roared as long as lungs could roar
Then quoth the Stranger, vain is all endeavour;
Sans voice to call sans vigour to pursue
And since your hat, of course, is gone for ever
I'll e'en make bold to take your Wig–Adieu

111. THE HUMANE GENERAL

Pen and watercolor; 7⅛" x 9⅝"
Inscribed verso: The Humane General / I. Cruikshanks [also on the verso a pencil sketch of three figures]
Published: July 13, 1801, by Laurie and Whittle
Not in George; impression in WMC

Two men stand in the center; one opens his shirt to display chest wounds, and the other points to wounds on his left arm. To the left stand soldiers at attention and two boys with fife and muffled drum. To the right a general, mounted, makes a compassionate gesture. The profile of the general bears some resemblance to that

110. THE WIG AND THE WAGS

of Wellington, but it is unlikely any connection was intended. He was at the time serving in India and had not yet risen to a position of great prominence.

Below the print are engraved some lines relating how two old soldiers sentenced to be shot for a breach of discipline gained a pardon when they showed their battle scars to the general in command.

112. SMOTHERING A RABBIT WITH ONIONS

Pen and watercolor; 7⅛″ x 9½″
Inscribed verso: Rabbit smothered with Onions / I. Cruikshanks
Published: November 23, 1801, by Laurie and Whittle
Not in George; impression in WMC

A young girl drops an apron laden with onions as a rabbit runs across the floor in front of her. An old man on crutches speaks to her, gesturing with the crutch in his right hand.

Beneath the picture on the print is engraved:
Sally, Sally what are you about, where is my Supper; where is the Rabbit smothered with Onions which I order'd an hour ago—Lord Sir I have been smothering it this half hour, till I'm in such a Broiling heat you might wring my Shirt—I have thrown all the onions in the House over it twenty times, and he don't mind it at all—only see how he gallops about the kitchen as if he had been used to smothering all his life.

113. UNFORTUNATE MISS BAILEY

Pen and watercolor; 6½″ x 8⅞″
Inscribed verso: Song of Miss Bailey / about 1803
Published: February 12, 1804, by Laurie and Whittle
Not in George (and not to be confused with George 10938); impression in WMC
Acquired: 1962 (not part of the Huntington folio volume of Cruikshank drawings)

A man, in his shirt and nightcap, sits up in bed looking at a ghostly figure of a woman with a cord tied around her neck. He holds a pound note in his hand. She gestures toward him. A small round table with a lighted candle, decanter, and glass stands beside the bed.

On the print is engraved the information:
Sung by Mr Matthews, at the Haymarket, and Mr Fawcet, at Covent Garden: In "Love Laughs at Locksmiths."

The verses relate the story of a Miss Bailey who hanged herself after being seduced by a captain. Her ghost haunts the captain, who agrees to bribe the sexton with a pound note to bury her corpse.

Isaac, probably in cooperation with George, treated

112. SMOTHERING A RABBIT WITH ONIONS

this theme again, with a different story, in 1807 (George 10938).

114. BOND STREET BUCKS & KEEN COUNTRYMAN

Pen and watercolor; 6¾″ x 8⅜″
Published: August 20, 1804, by Laurie and Whittle; numbered 364
George 10356
Acquired: 1959. (This drawing was not contained in the folio volume of Cruikshank sketches but was acquired independently by the Huntington Art Gallery with the Gilbert Davis Collection.)

Two fashionably dressed young men parade to the left along Bond Street. A countryman eyes them from the right.

On the print beneath the title is engraved:
Two Bond Street loungers discoursing in Piccadilly, one of them said, he wish'd much to go into the Country, upon which the other made the following observation:
In the Country, my Friend there is nought to be seen,
But an Ass on a Common, or a Goose on a Green.

A countryman passing at the time, pronounced the following impromptu:
There would be in the Country them things to be seen
Were you on a Common your Friend on a Green

Appendix

The following are included in the Huntington album of drawings by Isaac Cruikshank but are designated by George Cruikshank as not by his father. All were published in the Drolls of Sayer or Laurie and Whittle.

The Corn Doctor	November 20, 1793	George 8409
A Maiden Ewe	September 15, 1796	Not in George (LWL)
Tap-room Politicians	July 13, 1795	George 8773
The Patient turn'd Doctor	May 12, 1794	George 8580

114. BOND STREET BUCKS & KEEN COUNTRYMAN